Simply Nantucket

Simply Nantucket

Photographs by Amanda Lumry and Loren Wengerd

Written by Laura Hurwitz

All photographs by Amanda Lumry and Loren Wengerd.

Cover design, page layouts, and map illustration by Allison Doane.

First edition published 2006 by Eaglemont Press
PMB 741
15600 NE 8th #B-1
Bellevue, WA 98008
(425) 462-6144
info@eaglemontpress.com
www.eaglemontpress.com

ISBN-13: 978-0-9748411-9-9
ISBN-10: 0-9748411-9-6

10 9 8 7 6 5 4 3 2 1

Digital imaging by Phoenix Color USA
Printed in China by Phoenix Asia

table of contents

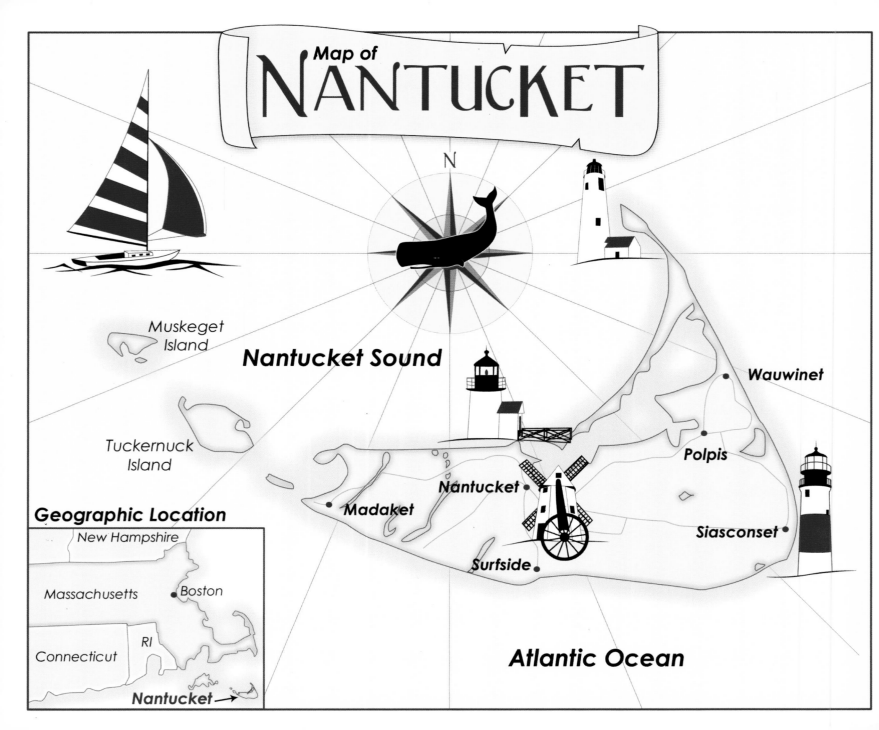

Map of NANTUCKET

N

Nantucket Sound

Muskeget Island

Tuckernuck Island

Wauwinet

Polpis

Nantucket

Madaket

Siasconset

Surfside

Geographic Location

New Hampshire

Massachusetts

• *Boston*

Connecticut

RI

Nantucket

Atlantic Ocean

acknowledgments

I want to thank the numerous island conservation organizations, including the Maria Mitchell Association, the Nantucket Conservation Foundation, the Nantucket Islands Land Bank, the Nantucket Land Council, and the Trustees of Reservation for their unflagging work. The beauty of Nantucket is a tribute to your efforts.

I would like to thank my parents, John and Frances Krick, for first falling in love with each other, and second, on their honeymoon, falling in love with Nantucket. Both loves have endured, and both have been faithfully passed down, generation to generation.

Thank you to the Tuttle/Noyes/DeWitt families, especially Grace, Isabelle, and Harriet, for sharing your amazing home and many insights.

Thank you to those we met along the way. Many had a hand in putting this book together, and we truly could not have completed this journey without you.

introduction

Nantucket is a Native American word meaning "The Faraway Island." Centuries ago, thirty miles out to sea was far away. Now, high-speed ferries and planes make this distance easily traversable. In an instant, cell phones and the Internet connect islanders to the pulse of modern life. Still, it doesn't matter that advances in transportation and technology have made Nantucket more accessible; the soul of the island resolutely maintains its distance. When you are cautiously navigating the cobblestone streets or watching the waves swell out in the vast Atlantic, life, as you know it, feels about a million miles away. Time stops here, caught in the fragrant tang of the salt air and the sonorous sigh of the foghorn. Nantucket is one Grey Lady who has not, over time, lost her mystery or her magic.

From its origins as a Native American settlement, to its colonization by a group of sheep-raising shareholders with such historically significant names as Coffin, Macy, and Starbuck, to its tenure from 1800 to 1840 as the whaling capital of the world, and from the Great Fire of 1846 which saw its sudden abandonment, to, its radiant rebirth as a cherished vacation destination, Nantucket has ridden out sudden changes in fortune as a ship might withstand fickle seas. Throughout tempestuous times, the spirit of Nantucket has persevered. There have been surface shifts, but the center holds. Cradled in the warm currents of the Gulf Stream, beach plums ripen every summer. Crowds swell and fade away. Rabbits and deer bound over the moorlands, and new cedar shingles weather in the sun, wind, and rain. The rhythm of every day, set into the constellation of every season, hums along. Always, there is the sea.

Nantucket stands on the threshold of the twenty-first century. Thanks to the prevailing, and passionate, interest in environmental and historical preservation, the cobblestone streets, original structures, and open spaces remain. Thousands of visitors come each year to watch the sun rise over the spire of the Old North Church and set on the beach at Madaket. They come for a day, a week, the season. Some never leave. The beauty of Nantucket draws them here and holds them under her spell.

Nantucket is, eternally, simply Nantucket.

sea

Nantucket Island is, literally and figuratively, shaped by the water surrounding it. Like a sculptor who is never satisfied, the sea is constantly reworking Nantucket's edges, powered by the tug of the moon and the swell of the tide.

The north side of the island faces the calmer waters of Nantucket Sound, while the rest of the island is bound by the changeable Atlantic Ocean. For centuries the port of Nantucket has buzzed with activity, though vessels bound for the Boston Tea Party, or ships hoisting anchor for year-long whaling expeditions to the South Pacific, have now been replaced by ferries, fishing boats, and yachts.

Nantucket is outlined by more than eighty-two miles of pristine white sand beaches. Every beach has its following. Families flock to the genteel Sound side waters of Jetties and Steps Beaches, where waves lap playfully at the heels of children constructing sand castles or splashing atop sandbars. Couples in search of a romantic sunset or a leisurely private beach stroll might be advised to head west to Madaket. Surfers and wave watchers might be drawn to the dramatic swells at Cisco, and those visitors craving a wider lounging-about beach, along with bathrooms, showers, and a full snack bar, would high-tail it to Surfside. Miacomet is double-edged; one side of the beach faces a freshwater pond, while a stone's throw away, the other meets the ocean. Whatever experience you are seeking, Nantucket has a beach for you.

Nantucket's connection to the water ranges from the practical to the transcendent. And whether you go down to the sea to look at the ships, play in the waves, or draw inspiration from its beauty, the water surrounding the island will not disappoint you. Calm or turbulent, the sea is the gently lapping or fiercely pounding force that has shaped, and still shapes, Nantucket.

Brant Point Lighthouse has been guiding ships into Nantucket Harbor since 1746.

Above, the *Eagle*, one of two ferries equipped to carry both passengers and vehicles, makes one of it many daily stops.

"Home is the sailor ..."

–A. E. Housman

"My favorite season in Nantucket is the fall. The water is still warm enough for a quick swim, and you often find yourself all alone on the beach. It's bliss."
–Nantucket resident

Steps to solitude

"Which beach are we going to today?"
—a common breakfast table question

Trodden trails to the sea

In Nantucket, even birds of different feathers flock together.

Nantucket Town Harbor: safely moored at sunrise

land

Nantucket is a diminutive sandy elbow of an island, just fourteen miles west to east and three and a half miles wide. But don't let its size fool you. Nantucket is packed with unparalleled ecological abundance. In fact, Nantucket boasts a greater variety of flora than any place of similar size in the United States. In the course of a single leisurely bicycle ride, one can pedal alongside beaches, dunes, pine forests, farmland, moorland, cranberry bogs, and open fields.

In addition to size, the other attribute Nantucket lacks is height–the highest elevation is Folger Hill, which soars a mere 109 feet above sea level–but you can visit one of the world's largest cranberry bogs on Milestone Road, and thrill to the variegated vistas across the Nantucket moors, which comprise one-third of the moorland in the United States–the largest moorland outside the British Isles.

On any given morning, from a spot along the curb on Main Street, the Bartlett's Farm truck displays its stock of fresh vegetables, fruits, and flowers. All are grown on the hundred-acre farm near Cisco, which has been operating since the early 1800s, and tempt the senses with their color, fragrance, and flavor.

Nantucket is still being developed, but with sensitivity to environmental impact and ultimate sustainability. In fact, more than 40% of the land on the island will never be built upon, thanks to the unflagging effort of conservation groups. Nantucket's open spaces will be preserved for future generations of hikers, bird-watchers, and artists.

Nantucket's beauty is legendary and, thanks to those who make it their mission to preserve it, eternal.

"I am on a mission to find the perfect red pepper."
–overheard at the Bartlett's Farm store

Nature's bounty

Home on Nantucket: picket fences, trellises, and cedar shingles, all aged to perfection

Tranquility amid the reeds on Long Pond

"Nantucket is the place that holds it all together for me."
–island visitor

Inland docks invite a range of activities,
from crabbing to contemplation.

Along Miacomet Pond

community

Nantucketers have a very strong sense of community. One glance at the *Inquirer and Mirror*, Nantucket's weekly newspaper, underscores their unity. Between community plays and church activities, musical concerts and yoga classes, swim lessons and storytelling hours at the library, the denizens of Nantucket keep both active and connected.

By far, Nantucket's most popular (and populous!) season is the summer. The year-round population of the island, roughly 4,000 residents, swells to over 12,000 during June, July, and August. Still, Nantucket never loses that small-town feeling of community.

Some annual events have become traditions, such as the Daffodil Festival Weekend, Nantucket's customary welcome to spring. Over three million daffodils bloom in a profusion of yellow blossoms throughout the island. There is an antique car parade, with vintage cars decked out with various themes, all in superb condition, as well as the annual tailgate picnic following the parade. Next, there is

Sandcastle and Sculpture Day in mid-August at Jetties Beach, where residents and visitors alike work on their sand masterpieces and are awarded ribbons in various categories. Then, in the fall, there is the Cranberry Harvest Festival, with tours of the cranberry bogs and samples of cranberry jellies, jams, and breads. Finally, there is the Christmas Stroll Weekend, with festively festooned trees on every street and carolers on every corner. Santa and Mrs. Claus even arrive on-island via Coast Guard vessel, and are escorted up Main Street in grand style by horse drawn carriage.

These yearly traditions provide a legacy of fun and anticipation, but Nantucket's true sense of community lasts year-round. Nantucketers are habitually independent, but they look out for one another. The sense of community is an extension of their love of their island and their fellow islanders. Their bond is palpable; you can hear it in people's morning greetings as you walk down the street, and see it in their smiles as they share the news of the day. Nantucket is a caring place.

Daffodil Festival revelers help usher in spring.

Summer is peak season for colorful, informal regattas.

54

"We are here for each other."
–Nantucket minister

Let there be peace on earth, and let it begin with me

Ringing in the Christmas season

NANTUCKET

history

Time marches on, but society's progress is somewhat less predictable. While many American villages reproduce a bygone era, Nantucket is one of the few towns that is the genuine article. More than 800 of the houses on the island were built in the eighteenth and nineteenth centuries; some, such as the circa 1686 Oldest House, built by Jethro Coffin, even earlier. With the sudden decline of whaling industry in the 1840s, Nantucket's residents were forced to seek employment on the mainland. Thus, while the rest of the country was swept up in the industrial revolution, Nantucket was left, intact, by the wayside. This sudden mass exodus proved to be Nantucket's salvation. Decades later, when artists in search of subject matter stumbled upon Nantucket's quaint charm, those who followed were similarly captivated by its unspoiled antiquity and knew to leave well enough utterly and splendidly alone.

While Nantucket has been described as "the place that time forgot", that would hardly be accurate. In fact, much of its beauty lies in the mark of time. The weathered shingles, the shady spread of the ancient elm trees at the top of Main Street, and the ruts in the cobblestone streets all reveal the rich patina of history. A visit to the numerous museums and historic sites provide added meaning and context. Visit the Old Windmill, still in operation, or wander through the now unoccupied cells at the Old Gaol (Jail), and you get a very real picture of life in Nantucket hundreds of years ago. Virtually everywhere you turn in Nantucket Town, you can see the past alive and well and living in the present.

Genuine antiquity is one thing, but history can be measured one day at a time in Nantucket. Time accumulates. Families return year after year, generation after generation. Nantucket is not immune to change, but unlike most places, obsolescence is treasured rather than torn down and reconstructed. Here, even the shortest passage of time creates history. From the maritime artifacts enshrined at the Whaling Museum to family photo albums documenting a week at the beach, all are testaments to the time, the history, and even the happenstance that have gone into creating this unique and beautiful island.

"*The past is all around you, and the wonderful thing is, it's still alive.*"
—overheard on Main Street

Cobblestones create a functional mosaic on Main Street.

Hand-held history

LUCY

WIDOW OF
Edward M Gardner
DIED
Jan.18 1875
Aged 55

SAMUEL P. LATHROP
Oct 20 1869
April 22 1943

"As you are now, so once was I ..."
–part of a popular epitaph often inscribed on Nantucket headstones

The Old Windmill on the corner of South Mill and Prospect streets has been grinding corn and other grains since 1746.

"*The past is precious here. People like me are committed to preserving it.*"
–local innkeeper

A profusion of wild roses frame the door to this quaint and uniquely named dwelling in Sconset.

The sweeping natural beauty of Nantucket is overwhelming, but when your pulse slows, look around. It is the small beauty, the delicate play of light and shadow, the purity in the commonplace, that ultimately captures your heart.

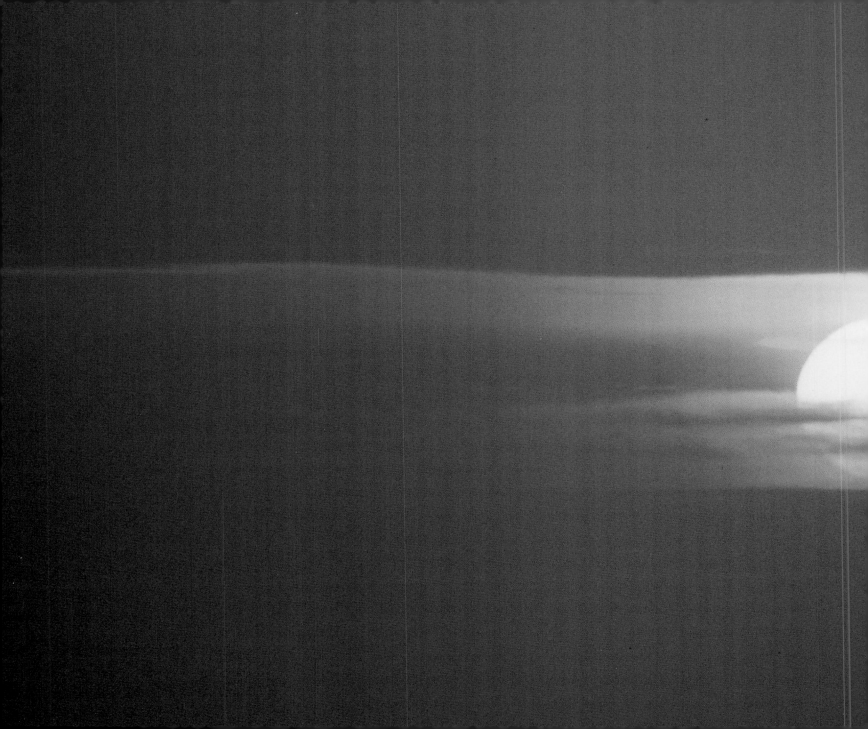

photo credits

i. Fence at Miacomet-**A.L.**
ii-iii. House at Madaket-**A.L.**
iv. Sankaty Head lighthouse-**A.L.**
viii. Beach-**A.L.**
2. Overlooking Town Harbor-**A.L.**
4. Brant Point lighthouse-**L.W.**
5. Beach-**A.L.**
6. Town Harbor with ferry-**L.W.**
7. The *Eagle* docked in town-**A.L.**
8. Town Harbor-**L.W.**
9. Sailboat-**A.L.**
10. Life preserver-**A.L.**
11. Buoy collection-**A.L.**
12. Shore by Smith's Point-**L.W.**
13. The steps to Steps Beach-**A.L.**
14. Reading at Nobadeer Beach-**A.L.**
15. Playing in the surf at Cisco-**A.L.**
16. Surfside fun-**A.L.**
17. Lifeguard chair at Madaket-**A.L.**
18. Dune grass at Miacomet-**A.L.**
19. Wooden footpath at Madaket-**A.L.**
20. Harbor from Washington Ave.-**A.L.**
21. Miacomet-**A.L.**
22. Town Harbor, yachts at sunrise-**L.W.**
23. Seagull-**A.L.**
24. Seafoam-**A.L.**
25. Gentle surf at Jetties-**A.L.**
26. Off the Madaket bike path-**A.L.**

28. Bartlett Farm's fields-**L.W.**
29. Sign to the farm and brewery-**L.W.**
30. Summer squash-**A.L.**
31. Assorted vegetables-**A.L.**
32. Grapes-**A.L.**, Pears-**A.L.**
33. Black-eyed daisies-**A.L.**
34. Across the grass in Madaket-**A.L.**
35. Picket fence in town-**A.L.**
36-37. Fenced hedge, Brant Point-**L.W.**
38. Miacomet home-**A.L.**
39. Swans among the reeds at Long Pond-**A.L.**
40. Crabbing dock at Long Pond-**A.L.**
41. The dock at sunrise-**L.W.**
42. Sunrise over town from New Lane-**A.L.**
43. Fence and trellis-**A.L.**
44. Water reeds by Miacomet Pond-**L.W.**
45. Miacomet Pond view-**A.L.**
46. Daffodil parade-**L.W.**
48. Dressed for the occasion-**A.L.**
49. Daffodil boots-**A.L.**, Daffodil wear-**A.L.**
50. Decal-**A.L.**
51. Car grill with daffodils-**A.L.**
52. Informal regatta, Jetties Beach-**A.L.**
53. Sailboat-**A.L.**
54. Sandcastle contest entry, Jetties Beach-**A.L.**
55. Bike rack in town-**L.W.**
56. Spring flowers for sale, Main Street-**A.L.**
57. Police Officers-**A.L.**

58. Cranberries-**A.L.**
59. Cranberries and basket-**A.L.**
60. Wreaths for sale, Centre Street-**A.L.**
61. Bittersweet-**A.L.**
62. Town crier-**A.L**, decorated tree--**A.L.**
63. Santa Claus arrives-**L.W.**
64-65. Mailboxes-**L.W.**
66. Faded decal-**A.L.**
68. Basement window-**A.L.**
69. Off Main Street-**A.L.**
70. Cupola in town-**A.L.**
71. Side street cottage-**A.L.**
72. Cobblestones-**A.L.**
73. Dockside crossroads-**A.L.**
74. Sankaty Head lighthouse, 'Sconset-**L.W.**
75. Boy and his ship-**A.L.**
76. Headstones at cemetery on New Lane-**A.L.**
79. New Lane Cemetery-**A.L.**
80. Old Windmill-**A.L.**
81. Historic home-**A.L.**
82. The Oldest House-**A.L.**
83. Svargaloka, 'Sconset-**A.L.**
82. Detail of door and basket-**A.L.**
83. Window-**A.L.**
84. Front porch, Centre Street-**A.L.**
85. Brant Point Sunrise-**L.W.**
86-87. Sunset-**A.L.**